AFGHANISTAN
the people

Erinn Banting

A Bobbie Kalman Book

The Lands, Peoples, and Cultures Series

Crabtree Publishing Company

www.crabtreebooks.com

The Lands, Peoples, and Cultures Series

Created by Bobbie Kalman

Coordinating editor
Ellen Rodger

Production coordinator
Rosie Gowsell

Project editor
Carrie Gleason

Project development, design, editing, and photo editing
First Folio Resource Group, Inc.
Erinn Banting
Tom Dart
Greg Duhaney
Jaimie Nathan
Debbie Smith

Photo research
Image Select International Ltd/UK

Prepress and printing
Worzalla Publishing Company

Consultants
S. Irtiza Hasan, Muslim Students Association at the University of Houston; Mohammad Masoom Hotak

Photographs
AFP/Corbis/Magma: title page, p. 5 (bottom), p. 22, p. 29 (left), p. 31 (bottom); AKG Berlin: p. 9 (top); Paul Alamasy/ Corbis/Magma: p. 8 (left); Alamy/ephotocorp/Dr. Suresh Vasant: p. 7 (right); Alamy/RHPL/Jack Jackson: p. 15 (top); AP Photo: p. 28; AP Photo/Tomas van Houtryve: p. 14; Art Directors and TRIP/E. Parker: p. 12; Art Directors and TRIP/C. Watmore: p. 29 (right); Art Directors and TRIP/R. Zampese: p. 18 (left); Araldo de Luca/Corbis/Magma: p. 7 (left); Ric Ergenbright: p. 5 (top); Ric Ergenbright/Corbis/Magma: p. 27 (top); Gamma p. 23 (right); Heritage images: p. 6; Historical Picture Archive/Corbis/ Magma: p. 10 (left); Doranne Jacobson: p. 3, p. 13 (right), p. 18 (right); Roland and Sabrina Michaud/Rapho: p. 16 (top); Seamus Murphy/Panos Pictures: p. 25 (bottom); Quidu Noel/ Gamma: p. 17, p. 21; Caroline Penn/Corbis/Magma: p. 20; Reuters NewMedia Inc./Corbis/ Magma: p. 15 (bottom); Rex Features: p. 13 (left), p. 23 (left), p. 27 (bottom); Patrick Robert/Corbis/Magma: p. 30; Ann Ronan Picture Library: p. 9 (bottom), p. 10 (right); Christian Simonpietri/Corbis/Magma: p. 31 (top); Stapleton Collection/Corbis/Magma: p. 8 (right); Topham Picturepoint: p. 4 (both), p. 11, p. 16 (bottom), p. 19, p. 24, p. 25 (top); UNHCR: cover

Every effort has been made to obtain the appropriate credit and full copyright clearance for all images in this book. Any oversights, despite Crabtree's greatest precautions, will be corrected in future editions.

Illustrations
Dianne Eastman: icon
MikeCarterStudio.com: p. 26
David Wysotski, Allure Illustrations: back cover

Cover: A young girl learns to speak Dari, one of Afghanistan's main languages, at a school in Kabul.

Icon: A yurt, which appears at the head of each section, is the traditional home of many semi-nomadic peoples. Yurts are made from wooden frames covered in thick felt, and are easily transported from place to place.

Title page: Girls dress in traditional Afghan costumes to welcome people arriving at an education conference.

Back cover: A dromedary is a type of camel with one hump. Camels have adapted to Afghanistan's harsh desert climate. They can survive on very little water, they have thick pads on their legs that allow them to kneel in the hot desert sand, and they can close their nostrils to avoid getting dust in their noses.

Published by
Crabtree Publishing Company

PMB 16A,	612 Welland Avenue	73 Lime Walk
350 Fifth Avenue	St. Catharines	Headington
Suite 3308	Ontario, Canada	Oxford OX3 7AD
New York	L2M 5V6	United Kingdom
N.Y. 10118		

Cataloging in Publication Data
Banting, Erinn.
   Afghanistan. The people / Erinn Banting.
      p. cm. -- (Lands, peoples, cultures series)
Includes index.
   ISBN 0-7787-9336-2 (RLB) -- ISBN 0-7787-9704-X (PB)
   1. Afghanistan--Social life and customs--Juvenile literature. 2. Ethnology--Afghanistan--Juvenile literature. [1. Afghanistan--Social life and customs. 2. Ethnology--Afghanistan.] I. Title. II. Lands, peoples, and cultures series.
   DS354.B33 2003
   958.1--dc21
                                                    2003001263
                                                    LC

Contents

The population of Afghanistan is made up of many different **ethnic groups**. The largest groups are the Pashtuns, Tajiks, and Hazaras. Within each ethnic group are different tribes, made up of groups of families with the same religious beliefs, ethnic background, or territory. There are many differences between these groups, but they have a great deal in common, including that most follow the religion of Islam. Their differences are often caused by geography. Steep, rugged mountains and dry, lifeless deserts create barriers between Afghanistan's people, isolating them from one another.

A changing way of life

Life in Afghanistan changed in the mid 1990s when the Taliban, a religious and political movement, came to power. To keep order, the Taliban introduced strict laws that dictated how people should live. These laws took away many people's rights, especially those of women and people who were not Pashtun.

In 2001, the United States sent troops to Afghanistan to fight against **terrorists** living there. With the help of the Northern Alliance, an Afghan group that opposed the Taliban, the United States and its **allies** overthrew the Taliban government. Since then, Afghans have regained some of their freedoms. Girls now go to school; women are allowed to work; new jobs are being created; and people who were forced to move to **refugee** camps in neighboring countries are returning to their **homeland**.

(top right) *This girl helps her family herd yaks in the north. She belongs to an ethnic group known as the Kirghiz.*

(bottom right) *Many Afghan men wear turbans, both as a sign of respect for Allah and as protection from the hot sun.*

4

Wheat farmers in the Hindu Kush Mountains separate the grain, which can be eaten, from the chaff, which cannot be eaten. The Hindu Kush is the country's main mountain range.

A father shows his son how to clean a carpet. Before they are sold, carpets are washed and brushed several times to remove extra dye and loose threads.

Archaeologists digging in Darra-i-Nur, a cave in what is now northeastern Afghanistan, discovered that people lived in the country in 100 000 B.C. They found the skull of a Neanderthal, or early human, as well as tools from about 30 000 B.C. In other parts of Afghanistan, archaeologists uncovered pottery and tools that are 4,000 to 11,000 years old — evidence that Afghans were among the first people in the world to grow crops and raise animals.

Arrival of invaders

Between 540 and 550 B.C., Cyrus the Great, the king of **Persia**, invaded Afghanistan and made it part of his Achaemenid Empire. People in the **empire** were allowed to keep their languages, customs, and beliefs, but they had to pay taxes and follow the empire's rules. Many people rebelled, but Afghanistan and the rest of the Achaemenid Empire grew stronger and more powerful.

Cyrus the Great leads his army through Persia.

Alexander the Great invaded Afghanistan from 329 to 326 B.C. He was met with fierce rebellions that often began in the mountains.

Alexander the Great

In 336 B.C., the Achaemenid Empire began to crumble as Alexander the Great, the ruler of **Macedonia**, conquered much of the empire's land. He established beautiful cities that looked like those of Macedonia, with **bazaars**, shops, offices, temples, theaters, and fountains. For this reason, the cities were called "fountain cities." The ancient city of Ai Khanoum, in northern Afghanistan, is thought to have been built by Alexander. The city had an upper town, which consisted of a citadel, or fortress, and a lower town, where people lived, worked, went to school, and prayed.

Asoka's rule

After Alexander's death in 323 B.C., his empire was divided. By 270 B.C., Asoka, an emperor from India's Mauryan Empire, controlled southern Afghanistan. Asoka established the religion of Buddhism throughout the region. Buddhists follow the teachings of Siddhartha Gautama, who became known as "the Buddha," or "the Enlightened One." The Buddha taught that people are reincarnated, or born again after they die, and that the way they behave in one life will determine what their next life will be like.

The Kushans

After Asoka's rule, many **invaders** conquered Afghanistan, and the country's ethnic groups struggled with one another for power and territory. Around 135 B.C., a group of five tribes from central Asia gained control of Bactria, a region that is now part of northern Afghanistan and the countries of Uzbekistan and Tajikistan. They united under the Kushans, one of the tribes, and conquered much of the rest of Afghanistan.

During the Kushan Dynasty, the Silk Road, a trade route that linked Rome and China, was established. The route passed through Bactria, and made Afghanistan a center of trade. Evidence of this trade, including painted glass from Egypt, bronze sculptures from Rome, and ivory carvings from China, were found in the eastern city of Bagram, the Kushans' summer capital.

Carvings of the Buddha show him sitting still to pray and think.

Around 300 A.D., the Persian ruler Ardashir took control of Afghanistan and founded the Sassanian Dynasty. By 714, Arab invaders conquered the land. The Arabs were Muslims, or people who follow the religion of Islam. Muslims believe in one God, Allah, and are guided by the teachings of his **prophet** Muhammad. The Arabs **converted** people in their conquered territory to Islam "by will or by sword," which means that they killed those who did not willingly change their beliefs.

The Ghaznavid Dynasty

In 962, the Turkic general Alptigin conquered eastern Afghanistan. He made the city of Ghazni the capital of the Ghaznavid Dynasty, which extended from India to Persia and included Afghanistan. The dynasty flourished, especially during the time of the third ruler, Mahmud of Ghazni. Mahmud was a strong supporter of music, art, and **architecture**. He built many **mosques** and palaces, and brought intellectuals, artists, and scientists to live and work in his court. After Mahmud's death, the Ghorids, from northwestern Afghanistan, claimed his territory and burned Ghazni to the ground.

Archaeologists believe that the Minaret of Mahmud III, in Ghazni, was built to record Mahmud's conquests. His name is written on the minaret in Kufic, an ancient Arabic script.

When Genghis Khan was born, he was named Temüjin. After he gained control of Mongolia in 1206, his name was changed to Genghis Khan, which means "Universal Ruler."

The destruction of Afghanistan

In 1219, the armies of Genghis Khan, a Mongol leader from China, invaded Afghanistan. They killed thousands of people and destroyed everything in their path. Afghanistan was destroyed again in the late 1300s, when one of Genghis Khan's **descendants**, Tamerlane, moved through the area with his armies. Like Genghis Khan, Tamerlane destroyed settlements, cities, and monuments, and killed thousands more people. He even built towers out of the skulls of people whose towns and villages he destroyed.

The Timurid period

Tamerlane and his descendants ruled for nearly 100 years. During that time, which is known as the Timurid period, poetry, art, architecture, and education flourished. Tamerlane introduced new trade routes, encouraged industry, and united different ethnic groups. Tamerlane's son Shah Rukh continued his father's work by building **shrines**, mosques, and *madrassas*, or Muslim schools, throughout Afghanistan.

Tamerlane wanted to control even more land than Alexander the Great, and died in 1405 while trying to conquer China.

Mughals and Safavids

Beginning in the 1500s, various empires struggled for control of Afghanistan. For more than 200 years, Afghanistan was caught between the Persian Safavid Dynasty, to the west, and the Muslim Indian Mughal Dynasty, to the east. In parts of the country, Afghan tribes also fought against each other for smaller territories. One group, the Pashtuns, gained power.

In 1613, Khushhal Khan Khattak, a Pashtun warrior and poet, began a rebellion against the Mughal Dynasty by encouraging fighting between the Mughals and Persians. While the groups were fighting, Afghan tribes gained more control of territory within their country. The rebellion ended in 1689 when different Afghan tribes had driven the Mughals and Persians out of most of the Hindu Kush.

Babur was a Timurid prince who founded the Mughal Empire. In 1526, he made the eastern city of Kabul, with its warm climate and beautiful scenery, the capital of his empire. This illustration from the 1800s shows Babur's tomb.

In 1747, after the Persian ruler of Afghanistan, was **assassinated**, the Afghans declared their independence. A Pashtun chief from the Abdali tribe, named Ahmad Shah, declared himself "the supreme ruler." During his 26 years in power, Ahmad Shah worked to unite Afghanistan's warring tribes so the country could become more powerful. He established a Muslim empire, and eventually expanded his territory into India.

Fall of the empire

The Pashtun tribes united under Ahmad Shah came to be known as the Durrani tribe. After Ahmad Shah's death, the council of chiefs who governed with him began to fight among themselves, and the empire crumbled. In 1826, the ruler of the Moohmadzai tribe, Dost Mohammad Khan, defeated the Durrani. He asked the British, who were his allies, for help in conquering more land. When the British refused, he turned to the Russians. The British felt threatened, and they invaded Afghanistan.

Dost Mohammad Khan and his son sit overlooking Kabul, in this illustration from the 1800s.

British troops prepare to enter the Bolan Pass, in Pakistan, on their way to invade Afghanistan in this illustration from the 1800s.

The Anglo-Afghan Wars

Britain's invasion of Afghanistan marked the beginning of the First Anglo-Afghan War, which lasted from 1838 to 1842. Another war broke out in 1878 and ended in 1880 when an agreement was signed that allowed the British to control Afghanistan's relationships with other countries, but allowed Afghanistan to rule itself. Abdur Rahman Khan took control of Afghanistan with Britain's support. Then, in 1893, he and Sir Mortimer Durand, a member of the British government ruling India at the time, signed the Durand Agreement, which set the boundaries of present-day Afghanistan.

Uniting the country

To unite the country, which had been split by fighting between ethnic groups, Abdur Rahman Khan took power away from individual tribes and created a strong central government. He and his son Habibullah, who ruled between 1901 and 1919, began to modernize Afghanistan. Habibullah introduced the country to western medicine, such as antibiotics and vaccines, western technology, such as **telegraphs** and telephones, and non-Muslim colleges.

Habibullah, who greatly admired the British, was murdered in 1919 by an anti-British group. His son Amanullah took control of Afghanistan, declared its independence, and invaded parts of British-ruled India. The invasion began the Third Anglo-Afghan War, which the Afghans won. Britain was forced to completely give up control of Afghanistan.

Modernization

For the next 50 years, Afghanistan was ruled by leaders who continued to modernize the country. Many people opposed their changes, which included **abolishing** *purdah*, a practice that separates women from the rest of society, especially from men who are not family members; allowing girls and boys to attend classes together; and introducing a **democratic** constitution.

The Saur Revolution

In 1973, with the help of the **Soviet Union**, Afghanistan's King, Zahir Shah, was overthrown by his cousin Mohammad Daoud Khan, a former prime minister. Daoud Khan became concerned that Afghanistan was too dependent on the Soviet Union for financial assistance. The Soviets had helped Afghans develop their country by building roads, tunnels, and an airport. As a result, Daoud Khan turned to other countries, such as Saudi Arabia and Iran, for support. This upset Afghan **communist** groups, such as the People's Democratic Party of Afghanistan (PDPA), who supported the Soviet Union. In April 1978, the PDPA killed Daoud Khan in a coup known as the Saur, or April, Revolution.

Communism and the Mujahiddin

After Daoud Khan's death, the PDPA took over Afghanistan and introduced changes that many Afghans believed went against the teachings of Islam. Many groups opposed the PDPA, including the Mujahiddin, or "holy warriors." The Mujahiddin believe it is their duty to spread the principles of Islam and protect the Muslim character of Afghanistan.

On December 24, 1979, Soviet troops invaded Afghanistan. The Mujahiddin fought against the Soviets, receiving financial support from countries such as the United States and Pakistan. The conflict lasted ten years. During that time, more than 1.5 million Afghans and Soviets died; more than 6 million Afghans fled to refugee camps in Pakistan and Iran; and more than 3 million Afghans were left homeless in their own country. The invasion ended in 1989, when the Soviets pulled out of Afghanistan.

A soldier takes down the Soviet flag at an army base in Kabul following the withdrawal of troops from Afghanistan.

An ongoing struggle

Problems in Afghanistan did not end when the Soviets left the country. Different parts of Afghanistan fell under the control of different ethnic groups, many of which still supported the Soviets, and the central government continued to follow communist ideas. In the meantime, the Mujahiddin began to **recruit** Afghans from religious schools in Pakistan and Iran and gained support in the countryside. In April 1992, the Mujahiddin overthrew the Afghan government, but fighting continued as groups within the Mujahiddin struggled for control.

The rise of the Taliban

A group of Pashtun students trained in *madrassas*, or Muslim schools, in Pakistan emerged to fight for peace in Afghanistan. They also wanted to restore Afghanistan's Muslim character, which they felt was lost during and after Soviet rule. They were known as the Talibs, which means "students of Islam." The Talibs formed a group called the Taliban. They were led by their *mullah*, or religious teacher, Mohammad Omar.

In 1994, the Taliban began to take control of several major cities in Afghanistan. At first, people welcomed the Taliban because they promised an end to the fighting, but the Taliban soon introduced laws that restricted people's rights. The Taliban said that the laws were based on the *Shari'ah*, or Muslim law, but their interpretation of the *Shari'ah* was very strict and often reflected their own tribal laws and customs, not the principles of Islam.

Opposition to the Taliban

Unhappiness with the Taliban grew, and various Mujahiddin groups united to fight against them. These groups became known as the Northern Alliance. The Northern Alliance was most successful in the north, where it prevented the Taliban from gaining control. Heading the Northern Alliance's fight against the Taliban was leader Ahmad Shah Masood.

Taliban soldiers guard a main road in Kabul, ensuring that people do not break the law.

The war on terrorism

Fundamentalist Islamic groups began to use Afghanistan as a training ground for terrorists. A Saudi Arabian named Osama bin Laden headed one group, Al-Queda, which opposed the United States, Israel, and any countries that supported them. Bin Laden is believed to have planned many terrorist acts, including the September 11, 2001 attacks in which hijacked planes were flown into the Pentagon, in Washington, and the World Trade Center, in New York City. Another hijacked plane crashed in Pennsylvania. Thousands of people were killed, and the World Trade Center was destroyed.

The United States asked the Taliban to tell them where bin Laden was hiding, but the Taliban refused because bin Laden had supported their government when other countries did not. This refusal prompted the United States to declare a war on terrorism in Afghanistan. The war was supported by the Northern Alliance and countries around the world. The Taliban was overthrown, but fighting continues in some parts of Afghanistan where people still support the Taliban and Al-Queda. Afghans are hopeful that one day there will be peace throughout their land.

Soldiers from the Northern Alliance arrive in Kabul on November 13, 2001, following the surrender of the Taliban.

Women had to wear chadris *in Taliban-controlled areas. They also had to wear shoes with soft soles so they made no noise when they walked. The Taliban did not want women to call attention to themselves. Women who did not wear* chadris *and soft shoes could be beaten, jailed, or killed.*

Banned by the Taliban

The Afghans lost many basic rights when the Taliban took control. Women were not allowed to go outdoors unless they were completely covered from head to toe, and men were required to grow beards. Anyone who disobeyed the dress code was arrested, put in jail, or killed. Movies, TV, music, games, and pastimes such as kite flying were illegal. Today, these laws have been lifted and people's rights are slowly being restored. Movie theaters are open for the first time in years, and radio stations are allowed to play music again.

The Pashtuns

The Pashtuns, Afghanistan's largest ethnic group, live in the eastern, western, and southern parts of the country. They also live in Pakistan, where they are called Pathans. There are many different tribes of Pashtuns, and most Pashtuns belong to the Sunni **denomination** of Islam. The other main denomination is Shia. The Pashtuns believe they are descended from Qais, one of Muhammad's followers who spread Islam through Afghanistan.

A code of ethics

Pushtunwali, which means "the way of the Pashtuns" or "the code of life," is an unwritten code of **ethics** that traditional Pashtuns follow. Other Afghans also adopted many of its laws.

There are nine main principles of *Pushtunwali:*
- *Melmastia* is hospitality. Every Pashtun must welcome visitors warmly.
- *Nanawati* means that people running from the law are allowed to seek refuge and shelter, and that people are required to offer it to them.
- *Badal* gives people the right to feud with families who harm them or a family member.
- *Tureh* is bravery.
- *Sabat* is loyalty to one's family, friends, and tribe members.
- *Imandari* is righteousness. It requires that people behave in a moral way.
- *Isteqamat* means persistence in everything that people do, from their studies to their beliefs.
- *Ghayrat* gives people the right to defend their property, their honor, and their family's honor.
- *Namus* means that men must defend women against danger at all costs.

Male family members and religious leaders gather for a Pashtun engagement ceremony. Female family members have a separate gathering.

Additional inhabitants

In addition to the Pashtuns, Afghanistan's main ethnic groups are the Tajiks, Hazaras, Uzbeks, Turkmen, Kirghiz, Wakhi, and Nuristanis. The Tajiks live throughout Afghanistan, as well as in Tajikistan. They live mostly in Afghanistan's northeastern mountains, where they work as farmers and herders, and in and around the eastern city of Kabul, the western city of Herat, and the central city of Bamiyan. In the cities, Tajiks work as craftspeople and traders. The Tajiks are sometimes called Farsiwans, which means "Persian speaking," because they speak Dari, a Persian **dialect**. Most Tajiks are Sunni Muslims.

A Tajik girl looks after her baby brother. Their family lives on a farm in the northeastern mountains of Afghanistan, where they grow wheat and fruit.

The Hazaras

The Hazaras live in the mountainous region of Hazarajat, which is in central Afghanistan, and in Kabul. Their homes in the mountains are made from mud and stone, and their villages are protected by high walls. Hazaras are believed to be descended from Genghis Khan's Mongol warriors. The name "Hazaras" comes from the Persian word *hazar*, which means "thousand," because Genghis Khan's army was divided into groups of 1,000 men. Most Hazaras are Shia Muslims, but some are Sunni or Ismaili, a branch of Shia.

Hazara women wear scarves called hijabs to protect their heads and faces from a strong gust of wind in Bamiyan, in central Afghanistan.

The Uzbeks

In the northernmost parts of Afghanistan are several groups descended from Turkic peoples, who came from central Asia to invade Afghanistan. The Uzbeks are the largest of these groups. They live on Afghanistan's border with Uzbekistan, as well as in Uzbekistan. Uzbeks speak Uzbeki, a Turkic language that can be heard in eastern Europe and in central and northern Asia. Most Uzbeks are farmers, and are well known for breeding Karakul sheep and Akhaltekes horses. Some Uzbeks are traders or craftspeople.

The Turkmen and Kirghiz

The Turkmen and Kirghiz are two other groups of Turkic peoples. The Turkmen live on the southern banks of the Amu Darya River, in the north, where they work mainly as farmers. The Kirghiz live at very high altitudes, in parts of the Hindu Kush Mountains where few other people live. They raise Karakul sheep, yaks, goats, camels, and horses. Both groups are semi-nomadic. During the spring and summer, they travel with their animals in search of grazing land, and in the winter they live in settlements.

(below) A group of Kirghiz pack up their camp near the Hindu Kush Mountains. Today, there are far fewer Kirghiz and Turkmen in Afghanistan than there once were. Many were forced to leave the country during the Soviet invasion.

(above) An Uzbek farmer wears a lungee, or turban, and many layers of clothing to keep warm.

The Wakhi

The Wakhi people live in the lower mountains of the Wakhan Corridor, which is in the northeast, and in the northern province of Badakhshan. Many historians believe that the Wakhi, who are Ismailis, are descended from Turkic peoples, but their language comes from Persian. Many of the Wakhi people's stories and poems have religious themes. Others tell about Wakhi heroes or teach people how to behave. One popular type of poem is the *bulbulik*, a three-lined poem that is traditionally sung by shepherdesses as they watch over their herds.

The Nuristanis

The Nuristanis live in the Hindu Kush, where they mostly farm and herd. Some also live in the Chitral Valley, in northern Pakistan. Homes in forested parts of the mountains are built of wood, one on top of the other. The homes are usually three stories high. **Livestock** is kept on the first floor; the second floor is for storage; the third floor is for sleeping and eating; and grain is **threshed** on an upper verandah. Nuristani homes higher in the mountains, where fewer trees grow, are made from baked clay to protect people from the harsh weather.

The Nuristanis have a very distinctive culture. According to one of their traditions, boys must shave all the hair off their heads, except for a small lock at the back. Legend has it that if the boys die at a young age, they will be led to paradise by this piece of hair.

Afghan refugees

More refugees have fled Afghanistan than any other country. So many people have left that neighboring countries were forced to close their borders. By the end of 2001, more than five million Afghans were living in refugee camps, mostly in Iran and Pakistan. Refugees also fled to countries such as Turkmenistan, Uzbekistan, Tajikistan, and India. More than 50,000 Afghans have applied to move to North America and Europe.

Since the fall of the Taliban, many refugees have returned to Afghanistan, but they have had trouble finding jobs and homes. Countries around the world are helping Afghans rebuild their cities and develop their industries so that more people can return to their homeland.

Families prepare to go to sleep in their canvas tents at the Qum Quishlak refugee camp in northeastern Afghanistan. Life in the refugee camp is difficult. Many families left their belongings behind when they fled their homes because of war.

Nomadic and village lifestyles

In Afghanistan's mountains, plains, valleys, and deserts, nomadic and semi-nomadic peoples move from place to place in search of water and grazing land for their sheep, goats, and other livestock. The sheep's wool is used to make carpets and clothing, while the goats are valued for their milk and hides, or skins, which are used to make tents.

Nomadic peoples

Nearly one-quarter of Afghanistan's population is made up of nomadic and semi-nomadic peoples, including some Pashtuns, Kirghiz, Wakhi, Turkmen, Nuristanis, Arabs, Baluchis, and Brahui. Arabs live along the border with Tajikistan; Baluchis live mainly in the southern deserts and travel between Afghanistan and Pakistan; and Brahui live in the Registan Desert, which is in the south, and along the southern part of Afghanistan's border with Pakistan. Years of war and drought, or lack of rain, have made it difficult for many nomadic groups to survive. Some have moved to larger cities to find permanent jobs and housing, and others have been forced to leave their country.

Nomadic peoples, many of whom travel in camel caravans, provide towns and villages separated by long distances or difficult terrain with news from other parts of Afghanistan.

Camel caravans

In the past, people used mainly camels to travel through Afghanistan's deserts and mountain passes. Traders carrying wool, gold, silver, and silk along the Silk Road had **caravans** that were sometimes 1,000 to 2,000 camels long. To encourage trade, kings built *caravanserai*, which were large stables where camels and their drivers rested at night.

Today, nomadic peoples use horses, yaks, and camels as they travel — usually from three to fifteen miles (five to 24 kilometers) each day. The animals carry food, blankets, tents, children, pots, pans, and small animals, such as chickens. A small group of men often goes ahead to find a place to settle. When a group stops, the women set up the tents, unload the supplies, and prepare the meals.

Nomadic peoples sell their livestock and homemade goods in bazaars, or they trade them for tea, sugar, vegetables, rope, matches, and other necessities.

A new yurt is often called an aq uy, *which means "white home." This is because the yurt's felt is often white when first made. As a yurt gets older and dirtier, the felt turns gray and the yurt is called a* boz uy, *which means "gray home."*

Nomadic homes

Tents are the most convenient form of shelter for nomadic and semi-nomadic peoples because they are collapsible and light enough to carry. Some semi-nomadic peoples have more permanent homes. During the summer, the Kirghiz live in yurts. Yurts are dome-shaped structures made of long reeds woven together and covered by large strips of felt. In the winter, the Kirghiz live in settlements, in stone or mud houses.

Living in a village

Around Afghanistan's main cities and towns are clusters of small villages. Most villages are made up of several compounds surrounded by high walls. A compound is a group of homes, storage buildings, cooking areas, guest houses, and pens for livestock. Each compound is usually home to one large family. Village homes are usually made from mud and straw, and have flat roofs where fruit is dried. People sleep on hammock-like beds or on mattresses on the floor.

Families in Afghanistan are usually made up of people who are related, but some families consist of people who have the same religious beliefs or belong to the same tribe. Many of these families formed during times of war, when people were separated from their relatives.

Marriage

Many marriages in Afghanistan are arranged when the bride and groom are still children. Parents decide whom their children will marry based on the other person's ethnic group, whether the person's family is well respected and earns a good living, and how happy the couple will be together. In addition, the groom's family looks for a bride who is hardworking and easy to get along with, since she may live with them after the marriage. A bride's family looks for a man who is strong, brave, and honorable. Today, it is more common for a man and woman to have a say in whom they marry, but they still need their parents' approval.

The bride price

Once a partner is chosen, the fathers of the bride and groom discuss the "bride price," which is money that the groom pays the bride's family as thanks for his wife. If the bride's husband dies or divorces her, she receives the bride price. Negotiating the bride price can take months, and bride prices are often very high. Some men must save for years before they can afford to pay them. While the bride's family does not give money to the groom, they are responsible for collecting the dowry. The dowry usually consists of household items, such as pots, pans, jars, blankets, clothing, carpets, and spices, that the bride brings to her new home.

(top) A bride, in the center, is surrounded by her female friends and relatives before her wedding. They help the bride prepare for the wedding and escort her to the ceremony.

Wedding ceremonies

The wedding ceremony takes place in two stages. During the first stage, called the *nikah*, the bride's father and the groom sign a wedding contract. The bride is not present. During the second stage, the *arusi*, the bride and groom exchange vows in front of a *mullah*, who leads the ceremony. After the ceremony, the guests shower the bride and groom with candy-coated almonds. Young boys play a game in which they try to gather as many almonds as they can. They believe that the more almonds they collect, the more likely it is that they will get married.

Life's beginnings

A baby's birth is a joyous time for Afghan families. First-born sons are welcomed with celebrations that last ten days. On the seventh day, which is called *Shab-e-shash*, the local *mullah* blesses the baby and whispers "*Allah-u-akbar*," or "God is great," and the baby's name in his ear. The baby's mother stays in bed during the ten-day celebration. On the final day, she goes to a public bath where she receives new clothes and is served a special soup called *humach* which is believed to give new mothers strength.

The end of life

Like other Muslims, Afghans believe that people return to Allah after death. For that reason, the death of a family member or friend is a time for celebration. Men who die are bathed by their male relatives in the presence of a *mullah*, and women are bathed by their female relatives. Once the body is washed, it is covered in a white sheet and taken to the mosque where people say prayers for the deceased. The person is then buried facing Mecca, the holy city in Saudi Arabia where the Ka' bah, Islam's most important shrine, is located.

A mullah says prayers for a woman who died in Ganikhel, a village in the northeast. On the first Friday, and 40 days after a person's death, the mullah will read special prayers at the mosque in memory of the deceased.

Women in Afghanistan

Men in Afghan society have traditionally been seen as leaders, protectors, and **disciplinarians**. Women have often been viewed as property and as people who must be protected from society, especially from men who are not family members. These beliefs vary depending on the region and traditions of a woman's ethnic group.

The rights of women

According to Islam, women have rights, such as the right to own property, to work outside the home, and to be independent. In Afghanistan, some groups have interpreted the *Qur'an* in ways that have led to different rules about how women should behave. *Purdah*, which means "curtain," is one example of a custom that is not commanded by the *Qur'an*. Many women in *purdah* live in homes with screens and high walls so that men who are not family members cannot see them. Some women have male guardians, called *mahrammat*, whose duties include accompanying the women when they go outdoors. A woman's *mahrammat* can be any male that she is not allowed to marry, such as a father, brother, or uncle.

Some denominations of Islam ask that women cover their heads to protect their **modesty**, but the wearing of a *chadri*, as many Afghan women do, is not commanded by the *Qur'an*. *Chadris* are long cloak-like garments that cover a woman's body and face. Women see through slits over the eyes. A law passed in 1959 allowed women to choose whether or not to wear a *chadri*, but when the Taliban came to power in 1996, all women were forced to wear one.

Today, some women in Afghanistan wear a hijab, *or loose-fitting scarf. Other women cover themselves more completely or wear no head covering at all.*

Women wearing chadris wait outside the Friday Mosque in Herat. In many mosques, men and women worship separately. During Taliban rule, women were forbidden from worshiping if they were not completely covered.

Women and the Taliban

Before Taliban rule, many Afghan women were adopting modern lifestyles. In cities, they wore western-style clothing and makeup, and they worked as doctors, lawyers, and teachers. When the Taliban came to power, they limited the rights of women. For example, women were no longer allowed to work, and they were not allowed to seek healthcare from male doctors, who were usually the only doctors left. Women with serious medical conditions were sometimes admitted to clinics or hospitals, but a *mahrammat* had to explain the woman's illness to the doctor, and the doctor could only examine the patient through a screen, without touching her. Many women died because they were refused treatment or they were not properly diagnosed.

Since the end of Taliban rule, many women have returned to their jobs as teachers, doctors, lawyers, and businesspeople. This woman teaches at a public school in Kandahar.

Women in Afghanistan today

Many women fought against the Taliban in secret, even though they could be severely punished for their actions. Some women organized special schools for girls, and some girls dressed as boys so they could earn money in bazaars.

Since the end of Taliban rule, women have regained many of their rights, including the right to an education and to work. Organizations and individuals are helping them gain even more freedoms. The Revolutionary Association of the Women of Afghanistan (RAWA) was founded in 1977 by an Afghan woman named Meena. Meena was murdered in 1987, but the organization still operates in Afghanistan and the United States, educating Afghan women and encouraging them to enter the workplace. Suraya Sadeed is an Afghan woman who now lives in the United States. Since the end of Taliban rule, she has opened medical clinics for women in Afghanistan and is educating North Americans about the difficulties women and children face in her homeland.

Babies in Afghanistan traditionally wear very colorful clothing made from pieces of wool and cotton sewn together in interesting patterns.

The style of clothing that Afghans wear often depends on the area where they live and the ethnic group they belong to. A common outfit for men consists of a turban and a *shalwar-qamiz*. The *shalwar* is a pair of baggy pants, and the *qamiz* is a long shirt. Women traditionally wear long dresses or skirts over a *shalwar*. Since the end of Taliban rule, people are wearing more western-style clothing, such as pants, T-shirts, and shorter skirts and dresses, especially in cities.

Regional clothing

Clothing from region to region varies according to the weather and the traditions of the people who live there. In northern areas, many people wear clothing made from fabric with red, blue, and brown stripes. Nuristani women wear pants made from red and white fabric, skirts with **petticoats**, and elaborately embroidered blouses that are sometimes decorated with glass beads or small pieces of mirror. Hazara women who live in central Afghanistan, where the climate is warmer, wear long, loose dresses to keep cool.

On your head

Some groups of Afghans decorate themselves with elaborate tattoos, and they wear fancy headdresses for weddings, festivals, and other special occasions. Many Pashtun women wear felt headdresses that are decorated with bits of silver, while the headdresses of Turkmen women are decorated with embroidery and beads.

Turbans are common in Afghanistan, but they differ from group to group and from region to region. *Lungees*, which are traditionally worn by Pashtuns, are turbans made from two long strips of cloth that are wrapped around a man's head. Enough material is left over for a man to wrap around his neck, to keep warm, or to protect his face from wind and dust storms.

Caps

Many men wear felt *kolahs*, or skullcaps, under their turbans. *Kolahs* are often decorated with embroidered geometric patterns that vary from tribe to tribe. Turkmen males wear box-shaped caps made from Karakul wool, while Nuristani men wear Chitral caps, which are made in northern Pakistan. They roll up the caps' brims in summer when it is warm, and roll down the brims to cover their ears in winter, when it is cold.

Warm coats

Many northern groups wear *chupans*, which are long coats that cover a person's body from the neck to the toes. The coats are made from cotton or silk that is quilted with thicker fabric or **down**. Pashtun men often wear sheepskin coats, which have warm wool on the inside, while many herders from nomadic groups wear wool coats with long bell-shaped sleeves in which they wrap their hands when they are cold.

A Pashtun trader in the Hindu Kush wears a turban and sheepskin coat to keep warm.

*A Turkmen boy wears a box-shaped cap embroidered with a geometric pattern. When he is older, he will wear a **lungee** like his father standing behind him.*

When guests arrive at an Afghan home, their hosts treat them with generosity and hospitality. They are seated at the head of the table, which is the position of honor, and served a meal made from the best possible ingredients.

Preparing to eat

Women are usually in charge of the cooking. They cook over fires fueled by wood or charcoal, or in outdoor clay ovens called *tandoors*, which are built into the ground. Men are usually responsible for the shopping. In cities, they visit bazaars and bargain for the best prices. In smaller towns and villages, people buy their groceries from donkey sellers. Donkey sellers are men who travel from place to place with donkeys pulling carts filled with food and other goods.

Mealtime

Most Afghan families eat two main meals a day — one in the morning and one in the evening. In the summer, it is common to eat outdoors. In the winter, people eat indoors on cushions called *toshaks* that are placed on a thin mat called a *diserkhan*. Tables are covered with a *liaf*, or square blanket, that hangs over people's legs to keep them warm. Diners are also kept warm by a charcoal burner, called a *manqual*, placed under the table.

Foods from near and far

Central Asian, Middle Eastern, Indian, and Chinese cultures have all influenced Afghan food. Merchants traveling along the ancient Silk Road introduced Chinese tea and Indian spices to Afghan cuisine. Many Uzbeks and Turkmen in the north eat a soup called *ash* that is traditionally eaten in Uzbekistan and Turkmenistan. *Ash* is filled with pasta, beans, and vegetables. Pasta is also a main ingredient in other northern dishes, such as *ashak*, which is a type of pasta stuffed with meat, cheese, and leeks.

Important ingredients

Most foods in Afghanistan are made with local ingredients. Eggs and dairy products, such as milk, cheese, and yogurt, are served at many meals. Soups are also popular. Teapot soup consists of a broth made with chilies and vegetables, such as carrots, turnips, pumpkins, spinach, leeks, beans, and eggplants. The soup is made in a teapot over a fire or on a stove.

1. manqual: *charcoal burner*   2. sandali: *table*   3. takhta: *stone or wood plate*   4. toshak: *cushion*
5. liaf: *square blanket*   6. balesht *or* poshty: *cushion*

26

A boy slices a cucumber so a customer can sample his fresh produce.

Halaal foods

According to the *Shari'ah*, Muslims can only eat meats that are *halaal*, or lawful. *Halaal* meats include lamb, beef, goat, water buffalo, and camel. Pork is a type of meat that is *haraam*, or forbidden. A butcher must slaughter an animal with one cut, so that the animal suffers as little as possible, for it to be *halaal* and must say "*Bismillah*," or "In the name of Allah," when the cut is made.

Kebabs

Kebabs are eaten everywhere — in people's homes, in restaurants, and in bazaars, where vendors sell them at stands. To prepare kebabs, people cut meat and vegetables into chunks and stick them on skewers. Then, they place the skewers on a charcoal burner or over a fire and cook them slowly to give the kebabs a smoky flavor. Kebabs are made of various ingredients, but the most popular ones are made of lamb.

Afghans traditionally eat with their hands, so a handwashing ceremony, called haftawa-wa-lagan, *precedes all meals.*

Naan

Naan is a type of flatbread served with every meal. People often dip their *naan* in chutneys, which are spreads made from fruits or vegetables mixed with vinegar, sugar, and spices. Sometimes, people dip *naan* in *shorwah*, a type of gravy usually made from lamb. As a special treat, *naan* is stuffed with potatoes, leeks, and other vegetables.

In cities, people buy fresh *naan* from bazaars each day, or they buy fresh dough to make *naan* at home. In many parts of the countryside, people bake *naan* in *tandoors*. The hot coals at the bottom of the *tandoor* bake the dough slowly.

The fresh naan *is so hot that a young girl cannot pick it up with her bare hands.*

Pilau

Rice is the main ingredient of many dishes. It is often mixed with fruit, such as apples, apricots, and mulberries, and nuts, such as pistachios and almonds. *Dampokht* is made from rice that has oil, curry, and other spices added to it. *Pilau* is a dish that combines rice with meat, vegetables, and nuts. There are many kinds of *pilau*. *Chilaw* is made with a large piece of lamb or chicken; *qabli* is made with raisins, carrots, almonds, and pistachios; *reshta* is made with eggs; and *kala-pacheh* is made with the head and feet of a sheep. Rice is also used to make a porridge called *kichri* or *suleh*, which has split peas mashed in with it. It is served with sour cream or *ghee*. *Ghee*, or clarified butter, is similar to oil. People who are sick often eat *kichri* or *suleh* because they believe it will make them healthy.

A young girl balances a sack of rice on her head. Rice is served with most meals.

Tea

Tea, served hot or cold, is the most popular drink in Afghanistan. Teahouses called *charkharas* serve many types of tea, including green tea, which is very sweet, and *chai* tea, a type of black tea that has cardamom, cinnamon, and other spices added to it. People usually drink green tea on its own, and *chai* tea with milk and sugar.

A man enjoys a warm cup of spicy chai **tea in a teashop in Jalalabad.**

Sherbats

A *sherbat* is a popular drink made with fruit, sugar, and water. You can make *sherbat* with an adult's help.

What you need:
• 2 cups (500 ml) raspberries
• potato masher
• bowl
• 2 cups (500 ml) water
• sieve
• sugar, to taste
• pinch of salt
• crushed ice
• pineapple slices

What to do:
1. Mash the raspberries in a bowl. Add the water. Soak overnight.

2. Pour the mixture through a sieve to separate the fruit from the liquid.

3. Add the sugar and salt to the liquid.

4. Refrigerate the liquid for 30 minutes.

5. Pour over crushed ice and garnish with pineapple slices.

Off to school

Khadija woke up long before sunrise, so excited that she could not sleep. Today was her first day at school. When the Taliban was in power, only boys were allowed to go to school. She and her sister, Tamima, were taught in secret by their mother.

Khadija had other reasons to be happy. Her family was together and safe, unlike other families who were separated during Taliban rule because people fled to other countries or were put in jail. It did not matter that Khadija and her family now lived in a cramped apartment instead of in their large, old house, which was destroyed during the war.

(top) Many buildings in Kabul, where Khadija lives, have been damaged by war. The city is beginning to repair homes, businesses, and roads.

Khadija wanted to surprise her family by making them a delicious breakfast of tea, *naan*, and chutney. She quietly picked up a metal bucket and slipped outside to draw water for tea from the well. It was a beautiful morning in Kabul. A few people were out on the streets, mainly merchants on their way to the local bazaar to sell their goods. Khadija still felt strange walking around Kabul without her *chadri*. She could not remember a time when she did not have to wear one.

Many things had changed since the Taliban left Kabul. Not only could she and Tamima go to school, but her mother, who worked in a hospital before the Taliban came to power, was about to start a job in a women's medical clinic. Khadija's father had already returned to his job as a professor at the Kabul University, a job he lost when the university was closed.

The market in Kabul fills later in the day as people shop for fresh vegetables.

Khadija filled her bucket with water, and ran home to find her mother and brother, Mohammad, already awake.

"Thank goodness you're all right, Khadija," her mother said. "Please do not sneak out in the middle of the night."

"Oh, Mother," Khadija replied, "it's morning. I only went to fetch water. I was going to make breakfast as a surprise."

Her mother smiled and kissed her on the forehead. "You can still surprise your father, sister, and grandmother. They haven't woken up yet."

Khadija watches with excitement as her classmates arrive at school.

While Khadija and her mother baked the *naan*, Mohammad played quietly in the corner with the kite he had made with his father. Just as the *naan* finished baking, the rest of Khadija's family woke up.

Khadija's mother rolled out their *diserkhan* and laid the *toshaks* on top. Then, everyone sat down to eat.

"Are you ready for your exciting day?" Khadija's father asked Khadija and Tamima.

"Oh, yes, Father," Khadija jumped in. "I can hardly wait to study reading, writing, mathematics, and science in a classroom with other children!" "I can't wait to make new friends!" Tamima added happily.

"I'm glad to hear that you're both so eager. I have a special surprise for you." He opened a cupboard at the far end of the room and brought out two pads of paper and two pens. "I bought these for you at the bazaar. They're a special gift for your first day at school."

Khadija and Tamima wrapped their arms around their father's neck and kissed him on the cheek. "Oh, thank you Father," they said together. Then, they were on their way to school.

Glossary

abolish To cancel or put an end to

ally A country that officially supports another, especially during a war

archaeologist A person who studies the past by looking at buildings and artifacts

architecture The science and art of designing and constructing buildings

assassinate To kill by sudden or secret attack

bazaar An area of small shops and stalls

caravan A group of travelers journeying together, often for safety reasons

communist Relating to an economic system where the country's natural resources, businesses, and industry are owned and controlled by the government

convert To change one's religion, faith, or beliefs

democratic Elected by the people

denomination An organized religious group within a faith

descendant A person who can trace his or her family roots to a certain family or group

dialect A version of a language spoken in one region

disciplinarian A person who makes sure that others behave in a proper way

down The fluffy feathers beneath an adult bird's outer feathers

empire A group of countries or territories under one ruler or government

ethics A set of moral principles or values

ethnic group A group of people who share a common race, language, religion, and history

fundamentalist Following a strict set of religious principles

homeland A country that is identified with a particular people or ethnic group

invader A person who enters using force

livestock Farm animals

Macedonia An ancient kingdom in southeastern Europe

modesty The state of dressing and acting in a proper, respectable way

mosque A Muslim house of worship

Persia The present-day country of Iran, to the west of Afghanistan

petticoat A skirt worn under a dress or another skirt

prophet A person who is believed to speak on behalf of God

recruit To persuade someone to join

refugee A person who leaves his or her home or country because of danger

shrine A small area or structure dedicated to a god or saint

Soviet Union An empire north of Europe and east of Asia, which, when it broke up in 1991, was made up of fifteen republics

telegraph A device that allows people to send coded messages over long distances

terrorist A person who uses violence to intimidate a society or government

thresh To remove the grain or seeds from crops

Index

1 2 3 4 5 6 7 8 9 0   Printed in the USA 0 9 8 7 6 5 4 3